A Day in the Life: Rainforest Animals

Piranha

Anita Gane

www.raintreepublishers.co.uk
Visit our website to find out
more information about
Raintree books.

To order:
☎ Phone 0845 6044371
🖷 Fax +44 (0) 1865 312263
🖳 Email myorders@raintreepublishers.co.uk

Customers from outside the UK please telephone +44 1865 312262

Raintree is an imprint of Capstone Global Library Limited,
a company incorporated in England and Wales having its
registered office at 7 Pilgrim Street, London, EC4V 6LB –
Registered company number: 6695582

Edited by Nancy Dickmann, Rebecca Rissman,
  and Catherine Veitch
Designed by Steve Mead
Picture research by Mica Brancic
Originated by Capstone Global Library
Printed and bound in China by South China Printing
  Company Ltd

ISBN 978 1 4062 1786 5 (hardback)
14 13 12 11 10
10 9 8 7 6 5 4 3 2 1

ISBN 978 1 4062 1880 0 (paperback)
15 14 13 12 11
10 9 8 7 6 5 4 3 2 1

British Library Cataloguing in Publication Data
Ganeri, Anita
Piranha. -- (A day in the life. Rainforest animals)
597.4'8-dc22
A full catalogue record for this book is available from the
British Library.

Acknowledgements
We would like to thank the following for permission to
reproduce photographs: Corbis **p. 5** (Science Faction/
© Norbert Wu); FLPA **pp. 9** (Minden Pictures/Ingo Arndt),
16 (Gerard Lacz), **19, 22** (Minden/SA TEAM/FN), **21**
(Minden Pictures/Konrad Wothe); Photolibrary **pp. 4,
23 scales** (Animals Animals/Jack Wilburn), **6, 13, 23 fin**
(Oxford Scientific (OSF)/Rodger Jackman), **7, 23 jaws**
(age fotostock/Darius Koehli), **10, 14, 18** (age fotostock/
Morales Morales), **11** (Oxford Scientific (OSF)/Paulo de
Oliveira), **12, 23 prey** (Animals Animals/Phyllis Greenberg),
15, 23 gill (Animals Animals/Zigmund Leszczynski), **17**
(Oxford Scientific (OSF)/Berndt Fischer), **20** (Oxford
Scientific (OSF)/Jan Aldenhoven); Shutterstock **pp. 23 oxygen**
(© George Toubalis), **23 rainforest** (© Szefei).

Cover photograph of a red-bellied piranha reproduced with
permission of Getty Images (De Agostini Picture Library/C.
Bevilacqua/DEA).

Back cover photographs of (left) a piranha fin reproduced with
permission of Photolibrary (Animals Animals/Jack Wilburn);
and (right) piranha teeth reproduced with permission of
Photolibrary (age fotostock/Darius Koehli).

We would like to thank Michael Bright for his invaluable help
in the preparation of this book.

Every effort has been made to contact copyright holders
of material reproduced in this book. Any omissions will
be rectified in subsequent printings if notice is given to
the publisher.

Contents

What are piranhas? 4

What do piranhas look like? 6

Where do piranhas live? 8

What do piranhas do during the day? .. 10

What do piranhas eat? 12

How do piranhas breathe? 14

Do piranhas live in groups? 16

Do people hunt piranhas? 18

What do piranhas do at night? 20

Piranha body map 22

Glossary 23

Find out more 24

Index 24

Some words are in bold, **like this**. You can find them in the glossary on page 23.

What are piranhas?

fin

scales

Piranhas are a type of fish.

Piranhas have **fins** and their bodies are covered in **scales**.

There are different types of piranhas.

Most piranhas grow as long as your hand.

What do piranhas look like?

Piranhas have round bodies, with big heads and large **jaws**.

Piranhas can be blue, red, yellow, grey, or black.

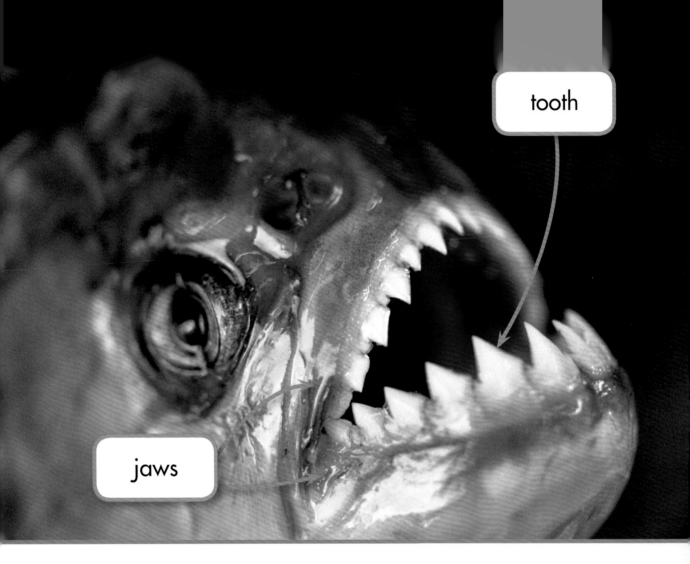

tooth

jaws

A piranha's jaws are packed with sharp, pointed teeth.

If one tooth breaks off, another tooth grows in its place.

Where do piranhas live?

South America

Piranhas live in the **rainforests** of South America.

It is warm and wet in the rainforest all the year round.

river

Piranhas live in warm water in rivers and streams.

If the water is too cold, the piranhas will die.

What do piranhas do during the day?

In the morning, the piranhas start looking for food.

They swim up and down the river hunting all day.

Piranhas have a very good sense
of smell.

They use smell to find out where
their **prey** is.

What do piranhas eat?

baby birds

Piranhas eat small fish, shrimps, and insects.

Some piranhas catch birds and lizards or eat dead animals.

Some piranhas eat seeds and fruit that fall into the water from riverbank trees.

A few types of piranha eat the **fins** and **scales** of other fish.

How do piranhas breathe?

Piranhas need **oxygen** to breathe.

They get the oxygen they need from the water.

gill

Piranhas have openings in their bodies called **gills**.

They take oxygen from water when the water moves through their gills.

Do piranhas live in groups?

Piranhas live in large groups called schools.

The piranhas stay in their schools as they swim, hunt, and rest.

caiman

Living in a school helps to keep the piranhas safe.

Animals such as caimans, find it hard to catch one fish when it is in a group.

Do people hunt piranhas?

In the day, some **rainforest** people go fishing for piranhas.

Then they cook them and eat them.

Rainforest people also use piranha teeth for making tools and weapons.

A pair of piranha teeth scissors is very sharp for cutting.

What do piranhas do at night?

Piranhas do not go to sleep at night in the same way that you do.

Instead, they save energy by resting in the water.

Piranhas stay in their schools at night in case there is danger.

Some schools rest close to the bottom of the river and others rest under plants.

Piranha body map

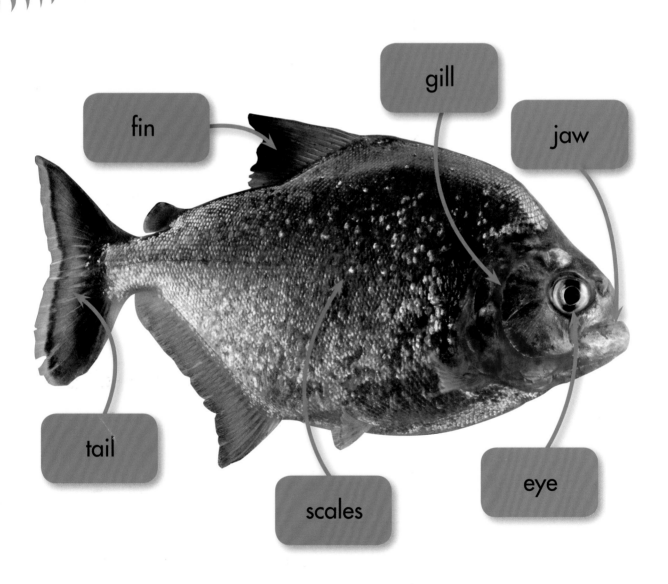

fin

gill

jaw

tail

scales

eye

Glossary

 **fin** flap of skin that grows from a fish's sides, back, and tail

 **gill** part of a fish's body that takes oxygen from water so the animal can breathe

 **jaws** top and bottom parts of the mouth

 **oxygen** gas in air and water. Animals need to breathe oxygen to stay alive.

 **prey** animal that is hunted by other animals for food

 **rainforest** thick forest with very tall trees and a lot of rain

 **scales** tiny, overlapping flaps of skin on a fish's body

Find out more

Books

Piranha (Extreme Pets), Deborah Chancellor
  (Franklin Watts, 2007)
Piranhas and Other Small Deadly Creatures, Tom Jackson
  (Crabtree Publishing, 2008)

Website

www.bristolzoo.org.uk/learning/animals/fish/piranhas

Index

breathing 14, 15
caiman 17
feeding 10, 11, 12, 13
fins 4, 13
gills 15
jaws 6, 7
prey 11, 12

resting 16, 20, 21
scales 4, 13
schools 16, 17, 21
South America 8
teeth 7, 19